A LITTLE PIECE

of

EARTH

Jean Mackie

Happen*Stance*

Acknowledgements:
The privately printed first edition of *A Little Piece of Earth* (1983) had a foreword
by Cuthbert Graham and was printed by Rainbow Enterprises in Aberdeen.
Jean Mackie expressed thanks in this edition to both Cuthbert Graham and R.F.
Mackenzie for encouragement. Acknowledgements were also made to *New Poetry*,
published by the Arts Council of Great Britain, *The Aberdeen Press and Journal* (for
poems published under the pen-name 'Mary Seaton') and to *The Scotsman,* which
first published 'Granddaughter'.

Printed by The Dolphin Press
www.dolphinpress.co.uk

Published in 2012 by Happen*Stance*
21 Hatton Green, Glenrothes, Fife KY7 4SD
nell@happenstancepress.com
www.happenstancepress.com

Orders:
Individual pamphlets: £5.00.
Please make cheques payable to Happen*Stance* or order
through PayPal in the website shop.

CONTENTS

JEAN MACKIE: POET, 1908——1991

My mother was told by her parents, when very young, that she would be plain. This was not wanton cruelty but a deliberate attempt to protect her from unsustainable airs and graces. In Jean's case it proved a self-justifying prophesy. She never did 'pretty' in clothes or make-up and no hairdresser was ever enriched by tarting her up. She wore sensible low-backed shoes, was large, rather than tall, at five foot nine, and she avoided cameras all her life. But that didn't hold her back.

She played hockey for the first eleven and was the first of her family to make it to a university, having scored highest in Scotland in Higher English. There she got an honours degree in English Literature and a circle of jolly, intellectual friends who stayed devoted to her as long as they lived. She later married journalist John R. Allan (author of *Farmer's Boy*), by common consent the best-looking and wittiest young man in the University.

Her citation in the *Biographical Dictionary of Scottish Women* records how "she founded St Nicholas School, Aberdeen, a progressive primary. Here she introduced a culture-starved post-war generation to music, dance, plays, books, poster paints and big brushes. Scottish Country Dancing replaced physical jerks, town children were introduced to cookery, gardening and animal care, and she once took 20 eleven-year-olds to the Bath International Festival (Beecham and *Ballet Rambert*) single-handed. She inspired her protégés with enthusiasm for the best things in life and expanded their imaginations."

The entry made no mention of poetry, and yet it should have. St Nicholas School dealt in Shakespeare, Milton, Burns and the folk poems of Scotland. She wrote musical plays for the children based on Homer and the Scottish ballads. The poems in

5

this pamphlet, all written in her sixties and seventies, provide a powerful interpretation of what she felt as an old woman. They are her only known poems.

Jean was the eldest of six children born to Maitland and Mary Mackie, tenant farmers of 400 acres at Tarves in Aberdeenshire. Five of the six made it to University but the ablest had to leave school early to be grieve at one of the outfarms added to Maitland's burgeoning farming business. Maitland was an old-fashioned Liberal, they say, but his wife was certainly a Tory. It is therefore a matter of some wonder to many that their six remarkable children, who were all intensely interested in politics, boasted three Socialists, two Liberals and one Communist.

The discredit (as his wife would certainly have had it) for this diversity, was Maitland's, and his vehicle was Jean. The old man may have done it just to annoy his wife, but he did spend quite a bit of time persuading his eldest that capitalism made no sense. Far better to have firms cooperating for the common good than competing for everything. And would it not be fairer that the workers should earn as much as the bosses?

Jean, in turn, worked on the other five. If old Maitland's mischief was designed to give him a good argument with and between his children, it certainly worked. The three boys all became Lords of one kind or another, including the one who left school at 15 to become a grieve. John Mackie became a Minister of the Crown and George became the Liberal Party's spokesman on Agriculture in the Lords. Mike, who tried for Parliament as a Liberal, became a non-political Lord Lieutenant of Aberdeenshire. Mary left the Communist Party in 1956 over the invasion of Hungary and became an honoured Labour councillor in Lincoln. And the baby, as Dr Catherine Aitken, for many years ran the Highgate Labour Party.

Always willing to laugh, Jean loved jokes and stories, but the thing many of us remember most is her use of laughter as an expression of welcome and of affection. That trait was reduced to absurdity when, in her old folks' home and advanced in dementia, she sat for hours with a similarly limited friend, listening politely to the other's chatter and laughing boisterously, though no-one else could understand it at all.

She was always good at parties—not the noisy kind where you had to dance and shout, but where wit was required. She enlivened the sticky part of an intellectual gathering in London by giving a demonstration of her low regard for housework: she showed them how to make a bed by getting into it and smoothing the various layers out, using her arms and legs in the manner of a swimmer doing an exaggerated backstroke.

After graduation she taught drama at Newcastle University, and worked on the *Express* in Fleet Street until she drew the line at interviewing a widow in order to get her to say how pleased she was she'd had her dead husband well insured.

Most of her writing was for the *Times Educational Supplement*, but she was also a contributor to the satirical magazine *Punch* and proud to have articles selected—twice—for *The Pick of Punch*.

In 1941, when invasion seemed inevitable, Jean and her girlhood friend, Margaret Wilkinson, managed to get the tenancy of an empty manse at the top of Glenesk in the Angus Hills. Their husbands were away at the war and they sought safety for their children and protection for themselves against the raping and pillaging expected from the Nazi hordes. I don't know whether it was one of her jokes, but my mother told me it wasn't long before the lonely young wives were taking turns to go to the head of the glen to see if there was any sign of the Germans yet.

Jean was a sensuous person. There were plenty of hugs in her family and she patiently undertook bedtime reading (*Pilgrim's Progress* and *The Odyssey*). She liked to run her finger tips over antique furniture, and her love of physical contact extended to the built heritage of the City of Aberdeen.

In 'To a poet who died old' she has the central character, (certainly her husband) scandalising people by embracing the stones of Old Aberdeen as he laid "his head against the walls in love". Slightly prudish about sex, my mother taught me about the bulls and the cows as soon as I had enough words to understand and infuriated me by always denying Santa was real, even after I had seen his boots at a Christmas party.

Jean told me that when you grow old you still want all the things you once wanted, and just as badly—only now you are less (and even un-) able to do them. I think that idea underpins most of these poems. Thus, in 'At the gates', Eve tries to tempt Adam to try some more of the forbidden fruit. When it's clear Adam has had enough, she says, "I want everything again, Adam."

When she was failing in the 1990s, I think I was closer to my mother than at any time since I was at her breast in 1939. Her only child, because of the four miscarriages which may have been her only profound disappointment in life, I visited Jean often in the nursing home and took my share of making the jokes and laughing unreasoningly. I sat with her for long hours, reflecting often on how people of her kind—left-wing, lapsed-Christian agnostics—would have questioned whether the humiliations were worthwhile (she raged against the nurses for what she thought were unnecessary invasions of her privacy; they took away her teeth to stop her biting her carers). She, who had read a book a day for most of her life, could no longer read. Most of those she loved were dead. What was the point of it all at that stage?

I think she saw me wondering for—perhaps it was her last lucid moment—she looked at me with an urgency and a certainty I had not seen for years and, taking my hand and gripping it, she said, "Charles, I want it all."

A LITTLE PIECE OF EARTH

ৡა

'*Some ants carry their young*
And some go empty
And all to and fro a little piece of earth.'

To
John R. Allan

Retirement

I sit in long contentment in his house
Wrapped in fire heat and sun heat,
The trees break the sun into long lines
Which cross the floor to meet
The steady warmth of the coal.
I lie on the old sofa,
A rug tucked round me by his gentle hands,
Was never lover's bed so surely warm.
I see him pass the window, bowed slow and sure,
Carrying plants, seeds, weeds:
All these he can still attend
But when he comes into the kitchen
He puts his hand on my head and says
The beasts are looking well.

Tomorrow, I say, *tomorrow I'll come and look*
Though I know
He sold them all a dozen years ago.

Granddaughter

When I was small my mother had to tea
Mysterious tall silk ladies,
All animation and affection.
That's how ladies were, I thought,
Sitting always among silver and small fluted cups
That were the colour of tussore silk
And sang like little bells.
It was my wedding china she would say
But two are broken
And there are no replacements since the war.

I had them both, in little pieces
Arranged on a moss green wall.

O, my loving innocent, my pretty dear,
Who sit now eating cake
Watching the ladies who have come to tea,
This is not my wedding china
Which was broken by the tenants in my war
And these large tweed-bosomed ladies
You think mysterious and tall
Are only Madge and Chrissie
With whom I played at the ball
And arranged bits of china on a moss green wall.

They huff and puff a bit now
And make statements that you and I
Think highly debatable.

But we do not debate.
All we are really saying is
We are Madge and Meg and Chrissie
Who played at the ball
And arranged bits of china
On a moss green wall.

Now Madge will read the tea leaves,
Tell you you will travel far.
She will not tell how deep her grief
To see your blind hands comb the sand
In search of pieces of your war.

Old woman

For sixty years you held up the house
With your strong body and stronger spirit,
Breakfast, dinner, tea and supper,
Weak morning coffee,
Port and whisky at the New Year,
Later, stronger coffee.
At the behest of your children
Wines you didn't know the names of.
You never needed any other stimulant
Than the breath of a new day.

They would not call you useful now
Since your whole purpose was to uphold one house,
Never any trouble for child or grandchild
But you were there,
Full of unrighteous indignation
Against the other side.

And sometimes you went quietly.
You made me a silk dress
One time my heart was broken.
There were eighteen buttonholes and a sash tie
But no comment,
No comment at all.

I used to watch your face filled with remembrance,
A hundred sweet cognisances
Running from the cage of your skull
Into the small spaces between bone and skin

And now there is no play of thought and memory.
Beautiful in decay as a caryatid
—Head free of the companionable stone—
Adrift across the lighted floor
You move
Perplexed
The strong house stands.

At the gates

ADAM Oh, Eve, I had forgot it was so still
That the blown trees would yet be lying
And the wild hyacinths growing by them.

EVE Quick, Adam, quick
There's a hole in the thorn hedge just here
And if I pull the paling wire so . . .

ADAM What then, my dear?
The Angel and his flaming sword
Wait at the other side.

Eve The sword will be rusted now
And the angel tired.

ADAM Not half so tired as I am. Let's sit here, Eve.
I'll take off my boots and cool my feet on
the waxy flower-stems.

EVE Adam, we'll get through, scattering the water from the cups
of the lilies of the valley.
Then in the raspberry canes to pluck
Our branch of the tree of Everlasting Life.

ADAM Eve, I'm not going flying in there in my old boots and
tattered fig leaves
Looking for everlasting life. I want no more.
Remember all that hiking in the desert after Moses,
Him with his stammer and his commandments?
And then there were the Crusades.

EVE At least you got a horse
While I stayed and minded the children.

ADAM   Just take note, I never asked about your friendship
               with the blacksmith.
        I always wondered why he joined the processions
               crying *Arms for Spain,* and then
               Support the Czechs.

EVE   He was at Aldermaston too, with anyone who cared.

ADAM   No, Eve, no more about the caring society. When
               the snow comes
        We'll build a little shelter and live quiet.

EVE   I want everything again, Adam.

ADAM   Cain and Abel, for instance?

EVE   Oh but they were sae fine when they were little.
        And you were a bonnie man, Adam,
        When first you issued from the Hand of God.

ADAM   That was just a painted lie.
        All guesswork, these stories. But I always liked
        The one about us hiding naked and ashamed
               among the raspberries,
        Pretending we didn't hear the word of God.

EVE   And us, staring at each other, so full of love and longing
        God could ha' burst his lungs calling and we not heard.
        Oh Adam, Adam, we can try again.

ADAM   Eve, Eve, Eve—is't not enough to remember
        How we turned and stood still among the harsh green
               raspberry leaves?

To a poet who died old

Did they, watching you, think
It is not seemly for this wild old man
To go out untended.
He should be combed and dressed
And urged to move
Neatly along the middle of the pavement.
He could take the air—what's left for him—
Fetching the messages
Or going to visit a friend not yet dead.
There is no more a challenge to that bright gaze.
He should not look so, nor walk uneven,
Nor lay his head against the walls in love.

Nor should he mutter.

Or did they know that murmur was within you,
A great cry like the shaking seas?

Here we walked
And here we stopped
And there the lamp shone through the trees.

Did they guess the truth—
You were not burdened by your age
But by your youth.

Revisitation

Do not take your love down the old barn stairs.
When you are old you will dream of the first places
And there's no room for sorrow there.

So we did not go.

She was a wise old woman
But how could she know
That most nights now
My love and I walk through the barn
And down the dusty stairs
And stand in shining straw
Clothed in delight?

The picture

He said *If you had bought the house*
I could have come to see you
Every day in summer.

She made a picture in her mind and hung it there
To think on after;
The frame of close-wrought boughs and flowers.
No fruit.

Sometimes she takes it down to look:
Pine needles prick her fingers, but
The young man and the girl have faded,
Loiter no more on the green paths,
Which still move upward to the stony mountains.

Circumspection

Let us walk with circumspection
In the village of our love.
Let us tell no-one,
Not each other,
That this is to last forever and ever.

Let neither catch the other's eye
In the schoolmaster's house
Lest our bones melt
And they know.
Let us not go entwined
But stay proud.
Let us not tell each other stories
Of our unhappy childhoods
But let us be thankful.

Let us make no plans,
Buy no rings.
After the concert
Let us walk away
Two feet distant
Holding the love between us
Lightly like an unregarded parcel

But even now we are accompanied
By the small sound of invisible feet.
The hundreds of dead lovers
Press about us, murmur their story
Without circumspection
In this ancient street.

The long days

Where have all the long days gone
When there was time for everything,
For love and sleep and walking
And even working?

There was time to plan the great lives we would have
And now we've had them.

Now I know
My father bought the food
And mother cooked it,
Our care was for ourselves
And theirs for us.
They had too little time for love and sleep and walking
But lots for working.

To the young

We do not envy you
The motor cars
The motels
The bedsits
The thousand worn divans.

We reached the lonely country on our feet
And dykesides did not creak.

Compulsion

They who had saved each thing they saw or heard or thought
And brought it home to the other
Had nothing new but sorrow to exchange.
Since each had to excuse the loss of love
There was no cruelty they could not compass;
The untied shoelace and the broken nail
Vied with the troops of the other's friends for hate,
The unfilled cheque stubs with the empty cradle.
There was no mercy, since they both were young.
She saw all this could translate into mourning.
But he, who had courted doom since he was weaned,
Could not connive at any kindly ending
So, the last unsayable thing said,
With what relief he reached
And pulled the roof about their heads.

Balcony scene

And suddenly she cried out
We must go in. We cannot sit here
In a stone balcony high above the street
With the sun hot on the table between us,
The youth peeled from our faces
And the dead past round our shoulders.
Do you not know that old men in the sun
Face the horizon, never each other?
It is not seemly to be here together
We are so changed.

You who sit there with your face in folds
Once kissed me in a rural summerhouse
And you must remember a whole flashing day
Planning a simple lifetime on the Kentish wolds.
Why do we sit here wearing painted hair
When time has taken all we once held dear?

In time they took her off, screaming of Helen of Troy.
The hostess said
And I had thought it would be nice to meet.

It wasn't said the host and slid
Heavily from the balcony to the street.

Tearoom

Sitting here I like it.
The waitresses are gentle, the coffee hot.
A new place,
I'm glad I found it,
Long narrow room
And the place where you are sitting feels your own.
It's easy to be here.

I am tired now.
You see I have to get up two hours earlier
When I am going to the town.
I used to manage with one hour,
Now I need two
In case I get flustered.

I like looking out at the young people passing.
How carefree they look.
We used to feel like that
Showing off our lack of years in the High Street.
Funny thing to boast about really.

Now I must take it slowly,
Put all my parcels in the big shopping bag
And the handbag in too
Because of the handle being apt to fly open
(I don't know anyone who mends handbags now).
First I'll take out the money,
I'll need my spectacles to read the bill,
Easy does it. I can't have lost them,

Mustn't spill mustn't fluster
Not let them know I'm not used
Not used not used . . .
Not used to my own town.
Oh let me not remember
How once benign the weather,
The rain darkening the stone,
The spring weeping in
And the blaze of summer.

Let me not remember,
Let me just work out the tip
And put it under the saucer.
Now I count the money into my left hand—
Oh but the bill I'm afraid I've lost—
Oh thank you so much.
Steady on, don't overdo it,
She didn't even pick it up.

Now the big bag in my right hand,
Let me move with apparent ease towards the desk.
There, that was simple really,
Now down the long floor—
Oh but the old sun blazes at the door.

Aberdeen awa

Some reflections on the fate of the Music Hall & other landmarks of Aberdeen

They have taken away my habitation,
They have taken my town.
I am an old man little regarded
But my grandfather subscribed to the Art Gallery.

They have made a study called *Gerontology*
In which they show that the elderly become confused
When the ornaments on the mantelpiece are removed;
So how do you think I feel
When they take away the Kirkgates
Upper and lower. It's like losing your teeth.
My grandfather, who died with every tooth in his head,
Cleaned them every day with salt and water
And subscribed to the building of the Art Gallery.

When I was young,
And I was young till I was sixty,
You could go back after ten years
And everything would be the same:
The flowers in Strawberry Bank,
The smell of the New Market,
The number of raisins in Kennaway's London Buns
And the old stone houses in the Gallowgate.

I am diminished when you take my past.

Every time I walk along a street my grandfather walked
And go into a shop in which all my aunties
Aired themselves and their most doubtful pedigrees
I am enlarged, I am sustained.

They tell me they are going to do City Centre Renewal
But they can keep their Walkway, keep their Complex.
I have my walkway in Belmont and Back Wynd
And down the Market Steps I had my Complex—
Small stone curves on the window tops
And the great roaring curve of the New Market.
When my grandfather had a drop in on a Friday
He'd walk across the babbling gossip of the Green
And stretch his arms about the walls and cry
Now here is the bravest backside in Aberdeen.

His affection for the Music Hall was more respectful;
Sober, he'd lead me in and tell me
The gentry had their parties here and now it's ours.
Ours is the double cube, the round, the square—
Of course it's shabby. Just you wait.
We'll have a Socialist Town Council yet
With money to conserve our heritage.

Hush, grandfather I said, and hush he did
To watch a woman dressed in white
Pretending to be a swan.

When you are old you can say you saw her.

It's true I saw Pavlova and now that I am old
Wait to see waterclosets in the Round Room
Dispersed amid the Corinthian white and gold.

I am an old man little regarded
With no teeth in my head.
I seek my dear familiars in stone,
The friends who comforted my youth being dead.

Poor Lady Macbeth

This is the time when the voices call me up
Out of my grave in the gentle Laigh of Moray.

Lady Macbeth, Lady Macbeth,
Tell us about yourself. We know
That you had little hands
Suckled your children
Bought perfume from Arabia
Loved your father
And liked a drop.

But why did you betray
Your womanly nature?

Please will you compare and contrast
The characters of Banquo and Macbeth?
And what about these witches and their nasty recipes?
Will you compare and contrast what they did to Macbeth
With what you did?
Egged him on, the lot of you,
Till you went mad and died and caused him then
To utter a Soliloquy
Which the teacher says is too beautiful
Too much quoted to quote.
So if everything has been said and quoted
What is there left to say and quote?

Whats more
We dont have to do the Shakespeare question now
But the teachers are so used to you Lady Macbeth
They cant stop.

Sometimes they warn us
We may get questions showing the New Approach.
Like

      If you had to dress up and act Lady Macbeth
      How would you bring out her characteristics?

O Lady Macbeth for the dressing up part
Wed need also your vital statistics.

And then theres

      If shakespeare were alive today
      Hed write sexnviolence for the telly discuss.

And also

      How has the reading of the play affected your attitude
      To the moral order?

O Lady Macbeth, we dont care about no moral order
Just so long as we get through our Highers.
We wont bother you again
If youll just tell us, tell us, Lady Macbeth,
Why you behaved and talked so cruel.

Dear children, if I had not so behaved
There would have been no play.
Dear children, there is one answer to your question—
A poet dreamed me.

I shall go back now to my grave. The air
Nimbly and sweetly re-enchants me there.

Recognition

I did not believe we would grow old,
Did not know what you meant when you said:
The crumbling flesh will sometimes borrow
Grace from the growing spirit,
So each the other may always know.

Yesterday, in Albyn Place,
I stood, stricken—
You whose smile would stop the heart
Came by, flesh bitten to the bone,
And passed me with an empty face.

Curriculum vitae

Once I was a girl weeping on a rented bed.

Now I am an old woman
With two public rooms
And three bedrooms
All empty

And I cannot weep.

The shadow (he remembers)

I remember
You were lovely with little things,
Ducks in the park
And the children we met on the street.

A cold spring sun I remember
And a pond riddled with light,
The young ducks thrashing the water,
You standing deep in delight.

When we met with the children playing
You'd stand smiling,
Watching, waiting,
Then gravely conversing
And I'd stand by
Watching, waiting.

They tell me you are blind now.
There'll be a great store laid up
Behind those North Sea eyes.
Are the ducks there? And the sun on the water?
And the children playing?
Is then the shadow of a once young man
Watching, waiting?

On studying my address book

It was that Welsh girl who said
You are the perfect unfaithful friend.
You bathe in the love and laughter you create
And then you go away and forget.

I have thought since of the devotions neglected.
Sure there was all time left
In which to write, to visit, to invite.
Now deaths and distractions have left me
High and dry on doorsteps to which I am unknown.
I need not knock.

Now The Address Book is a Roll of Honour.

The stranger

I stood and held your hand,
Putting on as pretty a show as I could.
But no, I did not know you.
Thirty years since you said
And did I not love you once?
I said I was ashamed not to remember
But I would give you tea and cake.
You sat there by the fire,
Made all the excellent old jokes
And then turned and said
You look exactly the same
And I shook my head
So as not to hear my voice tremble.

If had known you were to die that summer
I'd have come over to your chair
And put my arms around the stranger sitting there

But I was too busy reminding myself
Of what is becoming in ladies of fifty.

The old soldiers

Lonely in the world
We wait for Armageddon,
Looking forward a little
To having friends and enemies again
In uniform so's we'll know them.

It will not be like that.

They'll catch us

In lonely rooms in our daughters' houses
To which we have been allowed to bring the clock
                                    and the mirror
—We look the same, don't we? Don't we?—
They'll pick us off one by one in odd places,
Letting one drop on the grass,
The soft grass,
Another outside the shop while the groceries spill
                                    on the pavement
—Still wearing our boyish faces.

The artifact

Shaped like a plant it was,
With thirteen little knobs of light
On wires as thin as harebells.
At a touch it shivered into life,
Sliding against the thick, unwilling air
Till all the shopworn people smiled,
Not for the urban oddity
But because
Sweet as molasses
Here was a toy for four pounds fifty
Could emulate the lonely grasses.

Family history

We three in the attic room
Speaking of the dead
As if it were the most poetical thing
To be dead,
To have your story finished,
To be the lad who gaed daft
When Leebie wadnae hae him
And went to California and died untimely;
To be the girl who loved the postman
Whom nobody else in the family loved;
To be the old lady who never forgot
The Boy who didn't write;
To be the boy who stood still
In the woods of Haddo
To hear the stable clock chime
And wrote of it after fifty years
To bring another old man to tears.

But now the large dead assail me,
Too new to accept their place.
They do not suit my picture.
They are raw. Some hate the others;
Others love without return.
Restless, they will not accommodate themselves.
I cannot arrange them
And the wind blows dust into my eyes.

Elegy

Strange, to weep
For a draughty tearoom in a cold town
And some young men and a girl
Who could talk about poetry.
There were better things, I knew then,
To do with young men
And I do not suppose
The talk was all that good

Nor witty

Nor were we all that pretty.

Suspicion now is certain
All golden lads and girls
Have looked like chimney sweeps
And carried clouds of glory on their brow.

Today I held the grandson of that girl
Who is dust now.